TORFAEN LIBRARIES
WITHDRAWN

Book No. 1728444

AMAZING Canyons
AROUND THE WORLD

by Gail Terp

a Capstone company — publishers for children

Raintree is an imprint of Capstone Global Library Limited, a company incorporated in England and Wales having its registered office at 264 Banbury Road, Oxford, OX2 7DY – Registered company number: 6695582

www.raintree.co.uk
myorders@raintree.co.uk

Text © Capstone Global Library Limited 2020
The moral rights of the proprietor have been asserted.

All rights reserved. No part of this publication may be reproduced in any form or by any means (including photocopying or storing it in any medium by electronic means and whether or not transiently or incidentally to some other use of this publication) without the written permission of the copyright owner, except in accordance with the provisions of the Copyright, Designs and Patents Act 1988 or under the terms of a licence issued by the Copyright Licensing Agency, Barnard's Inn, 86 Fetter Lane, London, EC4A 1EN (www.cla.co.uk). Applications for the copyright owner's written permission should be addressed to the publisher.

Edited by Claire Vanden Branden
Designed by Becky Daum
Original illustrations © Capstone Global Library Limited 2020
Production by Dan Peluso
Originated by Capstone Global Library Ltd
Printed and bound in India

ISBN 978 1 4747 7468 0 (hardback)
ISBN 978 1 4747 8121 3 (paperback)

British Library Cataloguing in Publication Data
A full catalogue record for this book is available from the British Library.

Acknowledgements
We would like to thank the following for permission to reproduce photographs: iStockphoto: Fabian Plock, 13, 28, Robert Ingelhart, 18–19; Images: Andre Gie, 14–15, Bogdan Dyiakonovych, 1, Hayk_Shalunts, 10–11, kojihirano, cover, Marco Regalia, 17, Mark Dumbleton, 5, Patrick Tr, 9, Shane Myers Photography, 6–7, 30–31, SL-Photography, 25, vitmark, 26–27, Wenbo, 22–23

Every effort has been made to contact copyright holders of material reproduced in this book. Any omissions will be rectified in subsequent printings if notice is given to the publisher.

All the internet addresses (URLs) given in this book were valid at the time of going to press. However, due to the dynamic nature of the internet, some addresses may have changed, or sites may have changed or ceased to exist since publication. While the author and publisher regret any inconvenience this may cause readers, no responsibility for any such changes can be accepted by either the author or the publisher.

CONTENTS

CHAPTER ONE
AMAZING CANYONS.......... 4

CHAPTER TWO
GRAND CANYON 8

CHAPTER THREE
FISH RIVER CANYON........ 12

CHAPTER FOUR
COPPER CANYON 16

CHAPTER FIVE
YARLUNG TSANGPO 20

CHAPTER SIX
COLCA CANYON 24

Glossary 28
Top Canyons to visit............ 29
Activity 30
Find out more 32
Index 32

CHAPTER 1

AMAZING Canyons

Canyons are deep valleys of rock. They reach far into Earth's **crust**, and can be wide or narrow.

Most canyons are made by rivers flowing over rock. The moving water cuts away sand. It also moves large pieces of stone. This shapes the rock over time to form a canyon. This process takes millions of years.

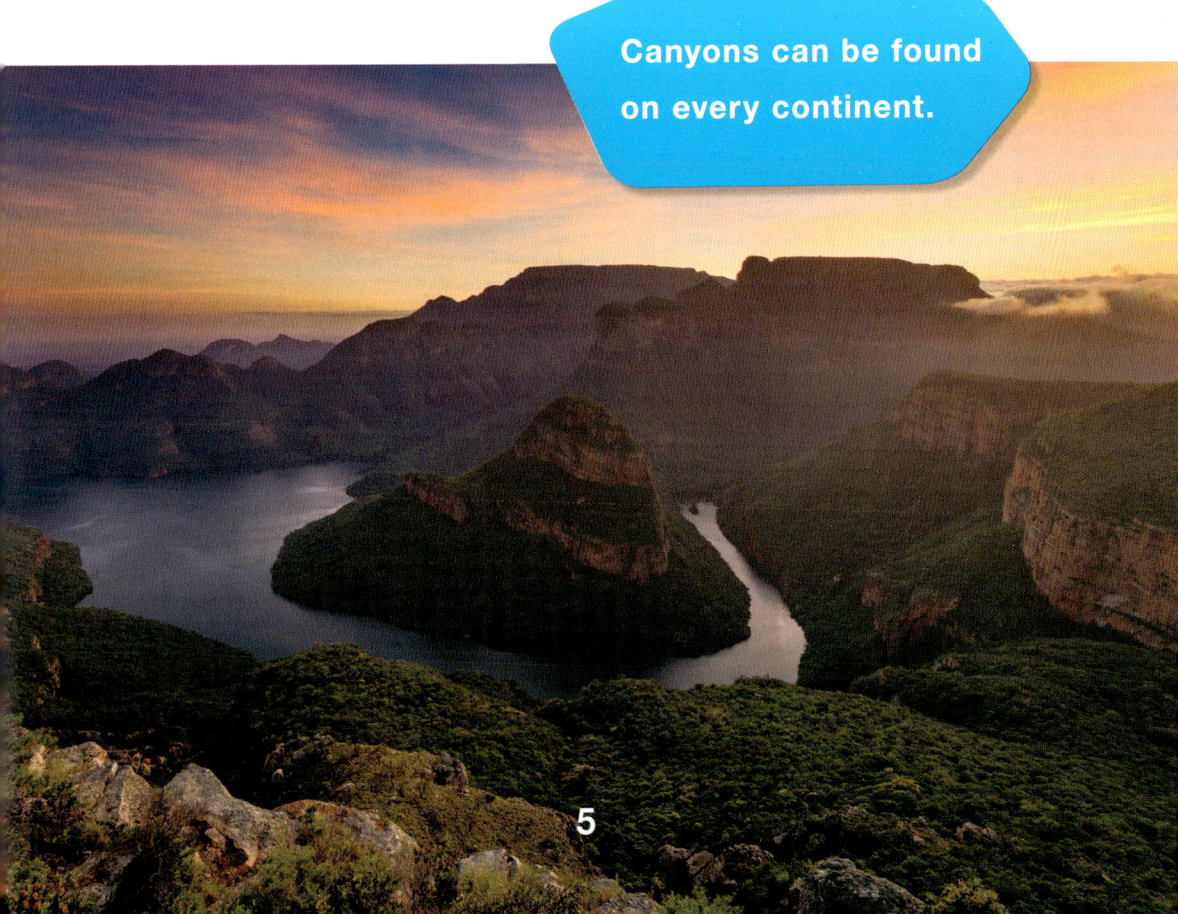

Canyons can be found on every continent.

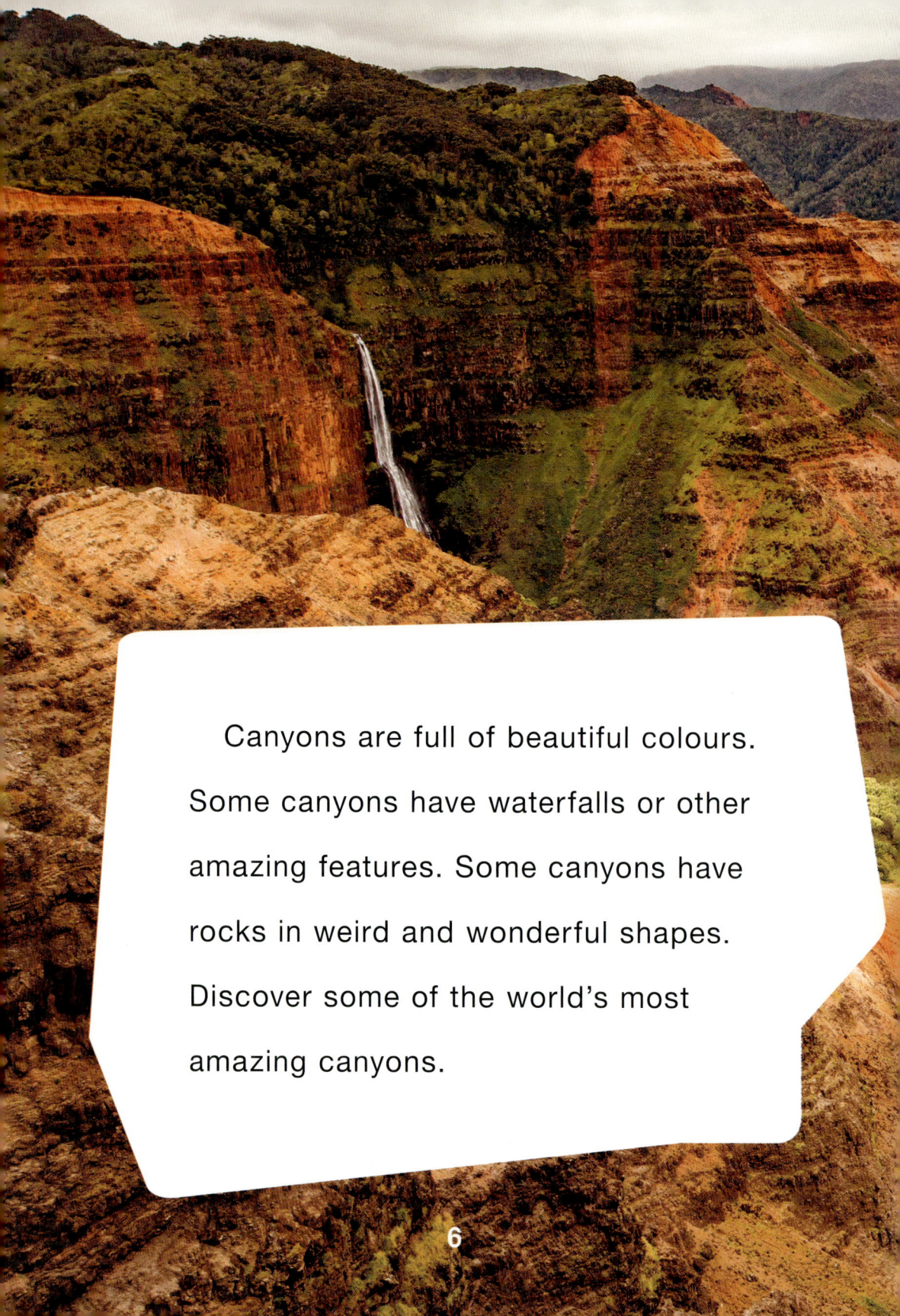

Canyons are full of beautiful colours. Some canyons have waterfalls or other amazing features. Some canyons have rocks in weird and wonderful shapes. Discover some of the world's most amazing canyons.

CHAPTER 2

GRAND Canyon

The Grand Canyon is in Arizona, USA. It is 446 kilometres (277 miles) long. Some parts are more than 1.6 kilometres (1 mile) deep. The Colorado River, and the streams that flow from it, shaped the Grand Canyon.

The layers of rock in the Grand Canyon are red, green and violet.

At its widest, the Grand Canyon is more than 29 kilometres (18 miles) across.

The Grand Canyon Skywalk was opened in 2007.

Visitors can go onto the Grand Canyon Skywalk. It is a glass bridge that sticks out 21 metres (70 feet) from the **rim** of the canyon. Visitors get a great view from the skywalk!

HAVASU FALLS

Havasu Falls is in the Grand Canyon. It is 24 metres (80 feet) tall and has beautiful green-blue water.

CHAPTER 3

FISH RIVER Canyon

Fish River Canyon is in Namibia. It is the longest canyon in Africa. It is 160 kilometres (100 miles) long, and 550 metres (1,800 feet) deep.

Fish River is usually just a small stream. But this changes during heavy rains. Then the river floods.

Fish River Canyon is millions of years old.

The hike through Fish River Canyon takes four to five days.

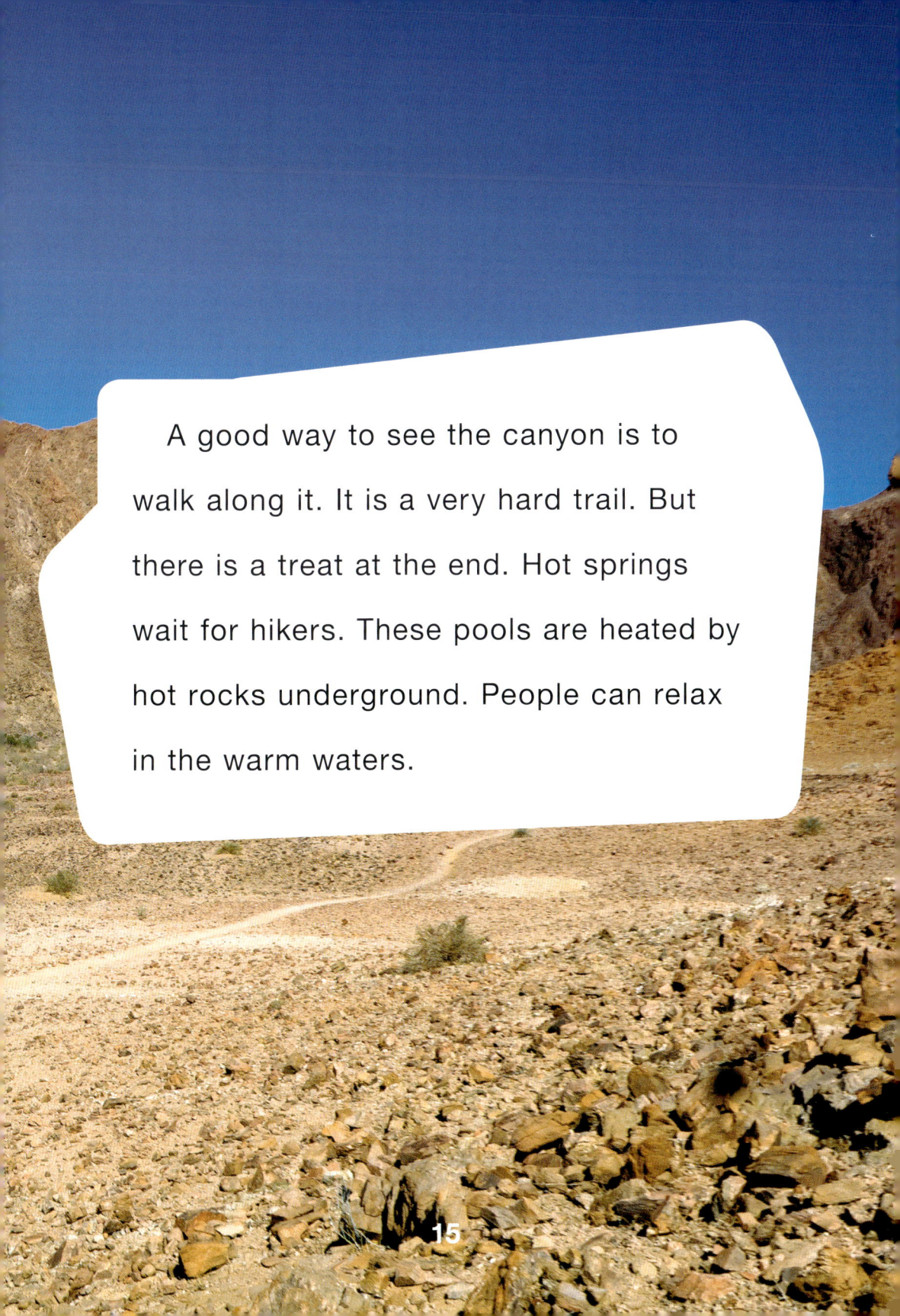

A good way to see the canyon is to walk along it. It is a very hard trail. But there is a treat at the end. Hot springs wait for hikers. These pools are heated by hot rocks underground. People can relax in the warm waters.

CHAPTER 4

COPPER Canyon

Copper Canyon is in northern Mexico. It is made up of six canyons. Each was cut by a different river. The canyon gets its name from the colour of its cliffs.

The canyon has some interesting rocks. The Valley of Frogs has rocks that look like frogs. Another valley has rocks that look like mushrooms.

Visitors to Copper Canyon can see the Valley of Mushrooms.

Visitors can travel on the Copper Canyon Train. It covers 640 kilometres (400 miles), and crosses 37 bridges. It also speeds through 86 tunnels.

The Rarámuri people live in Copper Canyon and farm the land for food.

Copper Canyon is home to **native** people of Mexico. The Rarámuri people live in the canyon. They have been there for thousands of years. They are known for being amazing long-distance runners.

RARÁMURI HOMES

The Rarámuri people are also called the Tarahumara. They live in houses called ranchos.

CHAPTER 5
YARLUNG Tsangpo

Yarlung Tsangpo Canyon is in Tibet. The Yarlung Tsangpo River formed the canyon. It is made up of many **gorges**.

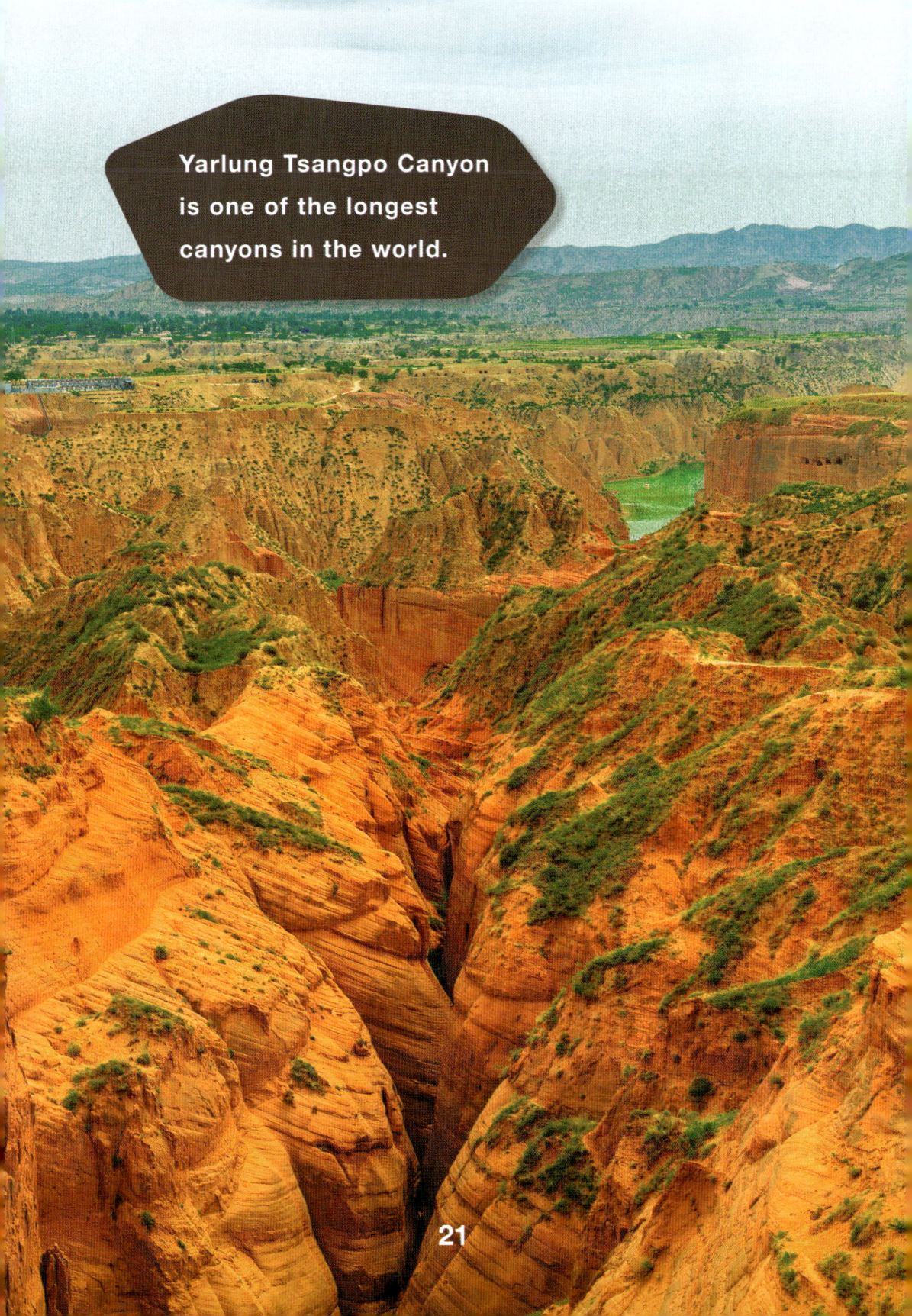

Yarlung Tsangpo Canyon is one of the longest canyons in the world.

The Yarlung Tsangpo Canyon is considered to be the deepest canyon in the world.

The canyon is 505 kilometres (314 miles) long. It is more than 5 kilometres (3 miles) deep in some places. That is deeper than the Grand Canyon.

HIDDEN FALLS

Hidden Falls is a waterfall in the canyon. It is more than 30 metres (100 feet) high. That's as tall as a 10-storey building!

CHAPTER 6

COLCA Canyon

Colca Canyon is in Peru. It is 100 kilometres (60 miles) long, and about 3 kilometres (2 miles) deep. The Colca River formed the canyon many years ago.

People live in the canyon. One group of people is the Collaguas. Another group is the Cabanas. They have lived there for thousands of years.

The Collaguas and Cabanas people farm and keep livestock in the canyon.

Andean condors make their nests on the canyon's cliffs.

Andean condors fly around the canyon. There is a lookout for visitors. The visitors can sit and watch the birds fly. These huge birds have a **wingspan** of 3 metres (10 feet). They can only be found in South America.

GLOSSARY

crust
Earth's hard outer layer made up of different types of rocks

gorge
narrow passage with steep walls that has a stream running through it

native
belonging to a place since its beginning

rim
rounded edge or border

wingspan
distance from the tip of one wing to the tip of the other on a bird

TOP CANYONS TO VISIT

COLCA CANYON, PERU
   Watch the Andean condors as they fly through the sky.

COPPER CANYON, MEXICO
   Buy a ticket and travel by train through this colourful canyon.

FISH RIVER CANYON, NAMIBIA
   Hike the difficult trails and reward yourself with a dip in a hot spring pool at the end.

GRAND CANYON, ARIZONA
   Step out onto the skywalk and take in the view of the Grand Canyon's colourful layers of rock.

YARLUNG TSANGPO CANYON, TIBET
   Take an exciting kayak trip down the Yarlung Tsangpo River.

ACTIVITY

MAKE A TRAVEL POSTER!

This book gives information about five canyons. For this activity choose one of them and do research to find out more information. Then create a travel poster about the canyon. Use bright colours and include fun information. Show others why they might want to visit this canyon.

FIND OUT MORE

Books
Canyon Hunters (Landform Adventurers), Anita Ganeri (Raintree, 2011)
DKfindout! Earth, DK (DK Children, 2017)
Valleys (Learning about Landforms), Ellen Labrecque (Raintree, 2015)

Website
www.dkfindout.com/uk/earth/rivers/colorado-river
Find out more about the Colorado River and the Grand Canyon.

INDEX

Andean condors 27

Cabanas 25
Colca Canyon 24–25, 27
Collaguas 25
Colorado River 8
Copper Canyon 16–19
Copper Canyon Train 18

Fish River 13
Fish River Canyon 12, 15

Grand Canyon 8–9, 11, 23
Grand Canyon Skywalk 11

Havasu Falls 11
Hidden Falls 23

Rarámuri people 19

Valley of Frogs 17

Yarlung Tsangpo Canyon 20, 23
Yarlung Tsangpo River 20